D0188876

Preparing Your
Family Business for
Strategic
Change

Craig E. Aronoff, Ph.D. and
John L. Ward, Ph.D.

Family Business Leadership Series, No. 9

Family Enterprise Publishers
P.O. Box 4356
Marietta, GA 30061- 4356
800-551-0633
www.efamilybusiness.com

ISSN: 1071-5010
ISBN: 0-9651011-9-3
© 1997
Third Printing

Family Business Leadership Series

We believe that family businesses are special, not only to the families that own and manage them but to our society and to the private enterprise system. Having worked and interacted with hundreds of family enterprises in the past twenty years, we offer the insights of that experience and the collected wisdom of the world's best and most successful family firms.

This volume is a part of a series offering practical guidance for family businesses seeking to manage the special challenges and opportunities confronting them.

To order additional copies, contact:
Family Enterprise Publishers
1220-B Kennestone Circle
Marietta, Georgia 30066
Tel: 1-800-551-0633
Web Site: www.efamilybusiness.com

Quantity discounts are available.

Other volumes in the series include:

Contents

The leader's job is no longer just to create strategy. The leader's job is to ensure that the organization stays fresh strategically. The difference is profound.

Once the business starts taking off, the factors that brought success tend to become institutionalized into a rigid strategy and structure. That dampens, not enhances, future growth.

Paradox: How you define your business and what brought it success determine your ability and freshness to see new ways to do business. A narrow definition of the business and its success factors can lead to paradigm paralysis.

We are the resource you can count on.

The Family Business Consulting Group, Inc.®

Tables

Exhibits

Preface

The purpose of strategic planning is not just to produce a document called a "strategic plan." The purpose also is to introduce a process of gathering information and thinking about it in particular ways, and reaching conclusions that become the basis for direction and action. The process is demanding of time, energy and teamwork. . . . But it does not have to be as painful as many business owners expect.

The genius of many entrepreneurs is their ability to pull together a successful strategy based mostly on instinct and passion. Many recognize a niche, single-mindedly go after it and prosper by their efforts. They may not check out empirical data. They probably haven't written a strategic plan. They certainly don't discuss strategy at directors' meetings (because start-ups are unlikely to have an active board). But make no mistake: Entrepreneurs have their implicit strategies and they can work very, very well.

Shorter life expectancy of strategies

Many family businesses have been able, in fact, to grow substantially without going through the time-consuming, sometimes emotionally threatening, process of explicit strategic planning. When the world changed slowly, explicit strategic planning was less important. Find a town that lacked a clothing store and start a clothing store. Build relationships with customers and suppliers and enjoy reasonable prosperity for a couple or three generations. A retail clothing store in a small town may have served its market well for several generations.

Then along comes a mass merchandiser, or perhaps, an interstate highway puts the store within 45 minutes of a regional shopping center. Transportation, communications and technology present many opportunities for new businesses and new ways for existing businesses to operate more successfully. But these advances also made it tougher to compete with companies that can invest more financial and managerial resources in keeping up with change. Few industries have been untouched. Retail, wholesale and other service businesses, the bastion of family ownership and operation for most of this century, have been particularly hard hit.

In the early 1900s, a business could follow the same strategy for perhaps 50 years and still enjoy success. By the 1950s, changes in technology and tastes shortened the strategic path to more like 20-25 years, which was mighty convenient in terms of generational succession. Just when a strategy was beginning to burn out, the owner might be ready to retire—the perfect time for the next generation to step in and breathe new life into the company with a new strategic direction. **As we look at the next generation of leaders in the family business, they will be required to develop new strategies as many as three to five times before passing the baton to yet another generation.** The strategic path from innovation through maturity to decline can be as short as five years. The skills and attitudes required to rethink the business strategically frequently differ dramatically from those of many past leaders.

This is not another book about how to do strategic planning. **It is a guide to help owners to view their family businesses strategically, whether the company is in its first or fourth generation.**

We seek to help readers view the business through a variety of lenses, so that family business owners can participate in the process of redefining their business. This is an important step in the process of creating a strategic culture that can recognize and adapt to changes that will inevitably affect the business and the family. Business survival and the family's commitment may depend on it.

The Family Factor

Strategies for family firms, unlike those of other businesses, can and should incorporate family factors. Family goals, needs, relationships and structure impact the business and its strategic direction. Family factors can energize, focus and build the business—or they can sap a business' strength. **Our experience with hundreds of family businesses has convinced us that responsible and disciplined strategic integration of business and family goals, strengths and values produces powerful results.**

This book will guide family business owners and their successors through the strategic business and family issues they need to identify and confront in the process of planning and implementing any strategy. Focusing on these issues will help family businesses maximize their inherent advantages and minimize the inherent disadvantages of running a family business. We hope to help family business owners and successors to think strategically. We will help to point out the skills needed to create a strategic culture that can harness the power of the family business' inherent strategic advantages.

"Responsible and disciplined strategic integration of business and family goals, strengths and values produces powerful results."

Part 1: Reaching Your Family Business' Strategic Potential

It is no longer the leader's job just to create strategy. It is the leader's job to ensure the organization stays fresh strategically. The difference is profound.

When Jim launched his first computer store 20 years ago, he had the skills and vision to unleash a long and exciting wave of success. Over time, he expanded his one location into a chain of 15 stores throughout the tri-state area. His two daughters and one son, now all in their 30s, joined the company and proved themselves to be very capable in their respective areas of sales, management and finance. However, the company eventually hit a bumpy plateau. Sales flattened, margins tightened. The founder felt that his tried-and-true strategies and tactics — so successful a few years ago — were no longer working. Challenges and threats, internal and external to the business, were becoming constant preoccupations. Family stress began to mount. What was going on?

Sorting through Mixed Signals

Business owners often wear two hats. Problems can be difficult to diagnose and decisions can be tough to call because business and family perspectives overlap. Table 1 illustrates some of the mixed signals Jim must weigh.

By separating the business concerns from the family concerns, Jim stumbled on many strategic issues that he never had to address before. The best approach for him depends on which phase his business has reached along what we call the *Family Business Strategic Path*. Understanding the developmental path family businesses typically follow may shed light on Jim's situation, as depicted in Exhibit 1.

Understanding the Family Business Strategic Path

In Phase 1, the founder builds a company from scratch around an innovative product or service. With a blast of entrepreneurial fervor, vision, energy and commitment, the founder engages in many trials and errors that enable the company to grow in fits and starts. And

TABLE 1

BUSINESS VS. FAMILY ISSUES

Business View	Family Business View
■ The company and its market seem to be maturing, which may require the business to take new risks.	■ As Jim approaches retirement age, he resists taking new risks that might put the business and his personal financial security in jeopardy.
■ New way of doing business and changing customer desires require new skills and new business plans.	■ New generations of family in the business have some of these new skills, but their commitment and vision are untested.
■ Jim has always made decisions unilaterally—he was the one who best saw the "big picture" and had the most information.	■ To prepare the next generation for leadership means to share responsibility, authority and sensitive information with the management team.

with the help of a little luck, the founder finds a "magic" formula that helps the company ride a comfortable wave of success.

As the business vaults past its startup period and into **Phase 2**, its leader appreciates that success came from more than a flash of inspiration. **The founder therefore tries to identify and define the ingredients of his or her successful strategy and installs a structure and policies to support it.** That strategy may sustain growth and profit in the intermediate term. But the danger of Phase 2 is that the founder often becomes married to this original strategy, which may not be responsive to the new demands of a constantly changing market. Eventually, this limits growth. It's better in this phase to appreciate that the strategic genius is temporary. **In the long run it's the whole organization that is responsible**

EXHIBIT 1 ▮▮▮▮▮▮▮▮▮▮▮▮▮▮▮▮▮▮▮▮▮▮▮▮▮▮▮▮▮▮▮

The Typical Family Business Strategic Path

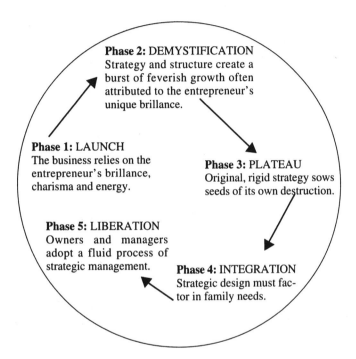

Phase 2: DEMYSTIFICATION
Strategy and structure create a burst of feverish growth often attributed to the entrepreneur's unique brillance.

Phase 1: LAUNCH
The business relies on the entrepreneur's brillance, charisma and energy.

Phase 3: PLATEAU
Original, rigid strategy sows seeds of its own destruction.

Phase 5: LIBERATION
Owners and managers adopt a fluid process of strategic management.

Phase 4: INTEGRATION
Strategic design must factor in family needs.

for success, not just the founder's brilliance. **Effective leaders in this phase deflect the credit and depersonalize the reasons for success.**

In Phase 3, **the business works harder and harder just to avoid losing ground. Profit margins erode because the company has already harvested the easiest, most profitable sales.** Many businesses bog down in Phase 3. Running a treadmill, they feel frustrated and discouraged. They've enjoyed a wonderful ride on a beautiful wave, but now they're paddling furiously to hold their own.

Before the original strategy fully runs this course, early in Phase 3 owners must identify their fundamental business strengths and competencies and learn to apply them in new ways. Here are two examples of companies facing these challenges:

■ A food products company began by supplying its local ethnic market, then expanded regionally. Thanks to new distribution ideas and creative marketing along with efficient production, the business successfully became a national firm. Now very large, the company's growth has slowed. Profit margins are shrinking. Generating new sales has become more costly. If the business is to maintain its multi-generational commitment to growth, new strategies will be required. While the company traditionally grew by emphasizing its products and brands, strategic planning helped the food products firm recognize that distribution had emerged as a core strength. Developing new products and brands for its distribution system became the company's new growth strategy.

■ Jim's computer outlets hit Phase 3 when the company exhausted prime store locations and consumers were buying more from discounters and by direct mail. The solution, which Jim almost ignored, was to start a field service organization that focused on helping schools and small businesses with repairs and new software installations.

Invariably, what worked in one set of internal and external circumstances may not work as those circumstances change. Jim ultimately realized (with input from one of his daughters and coaxing by his board of directors) that his original strategy had peaked. Typical of many leaders in Phases 2 and 3, Jim initially had a hard time adapting. Business founders tend to feel convinced that theirs is a sacred, winning formula for success. The problem is, they may not be sure precisely which parts of the strategy, structure and policies were most responsible for their success. Founders therefore may resist tampering with any part of their tried and true formula. Those who are able to challenge their strategic paradigm are likely to find a new wave to ride.

This is especially true as they reach **Phase 4**, when the next generation may come of age, with younger family and nonfamily employees joining the family business. Now **the senior generation leader confronts issues that challenge the company's ability to satisfy family as well as business needs. Family members may want money, jobs and a say in how the business is run.** Those new demands confront the founder, who is now typically stressed by flagging business strategy, the personal challenges of aging and concerns for personal financial security. Change is now needed to integrate the next generation's needs and goals and hopes. Change is also threatening to the senior generation as they contemplate the needs and fears of retirement.

Reaching **Phase 5 — liberation and renewal — requires that owners recognize the dynamic relationship between strategy and organizational design. They must challenge the reasons for success and explore new formulas and strategies as a regular part of managing. The strategic process becomes continuous. More than ever, this requires owners to champion change and to step outside the position where everyone looks up to them as the heroes with all the answers.**

TABLE 2

FAMILY BUSINESS STRATEGIC CHALLENGES AND RESPONSES

Evolutionary Challenge	Critical Leadership Response
Phase 1: Business is founded on entrepreneurial insight and energy.	LAUNCH Go for it!
Phase 2: Focused strategy and supportive structure generate excellent profits.	DEMYSTIFICATION Unbundle the reasons for past success.
Phase 3: The original strategy wears thin and inhibits change.	PLATEAU Challenge the current strategic paradigm.
Phase 4: Family factors begin to shape future strategy.	INTEGRATION Integrate family values, needs, capabilities and passions into strategy.
Phase 5: The business needs perpetual renewal.	LIBERATION Create a culture of change, a process of stategic management.

At Which Phase is Your Family Business?

Table 2 and Table 3 will help you find your place on the Typical Family Business Strategic Path.

TABLE 3

TYPICAL ATTRIBUTES OF THE FAMILY BUSINESS STRATEGIC PATH

	PHASE 1 LAUNCH	PHASE 2 DEMYSTIFICATION	PHASE 3 PLATEAU	PHASE 4 INTEGRATION	PHASE 5 LIBERATION
Leadership Values	Developing implicitly	Strong and Implicit	Strong and Explicit	Strong, Explicit and Contested	Subtle Adaptations
Core Com-petencies	Fragile	Strong but Implicit	Diluted	Uncertain	Renewed and Explicit
Strategic Infrastructure	Not developed	Developing	Rigid	Stressful	Flexible
Economic Value	Emerging	Growing	Stalled	Declining	Growing
Cash Flow	Business consumes most cash	Small	Increasing	Peaks	Adequate
Market Share	Increasing	Growing	Slows or stops	Stopped or declining	Rebou

Growth	Faster than market	Faster than market	Slows or stops	Stopped or declining	Rebounds
New Customers	Adding many	Gaining new prestigious customers, weeding out troublesome ones	Losing some good customers, replace with mediocre customers	Churning customers who become increasingly less profitable	New, good customers again
Strategic Spending	Large percentage of revenue	Decreasing	Cut back	Low point in new equipment spending, small increases on marketing, R&D, advertising	At a new high
Return on Sales, Investment	Hoping for breakeven	Increasing, especially gross margin	ROI plateaus, ROS decreases	ROI fairly high	ROI lower than Phase 2, but higher than Phase 3 & 4
New Products	Dominate	No new products	Increased breadth, but no innovative products	No new products	Rebound
Debt	Stretched thin	Declining (as a % of capital)	Not needed	Debt-equity at low point	Increasing

Note: for a graphic portrayal of financial performance over the family business strategic path, see Appendix I.

9

Getting to the Next Phase

Founders who tend to take personal responsibility for all aspects of the company — and who continue to rely on their own wit, energy and vision — have an especially tough time moving from one phase of their family business strategic path to the next. They feel their strategies are diluted or compromised by family interests. Some owners, though, see this time as an opportunity. Those who succeed in reinvigorating their company:

- do not feel as possessive of the business and its strategy;
- do not feel a need to know or control everything;
- trust that input from other people can help the business grow;
- recognize that change is not the enemy;
- view the business as powerful strategic entity with a life of its own, separate from that of the founder; and
- have a positive outlook toward their children as resources, not constraints.

Owners who agree with most of the above sentiments will have an easier time making transitions that go all the way into Phase 5—strategic liberation and renewal, where their companies can enjoy a new burst of energy and success by incorporating new ideas, and sharing responsibility and control.

Moving Forward

Clearly, getting from the early phases (relying on a rigid, personal strategy) to Phase 5 (staying fresh strategically as a management team) is no easy task. As we will see in the next chapter, the leadership requirements after the original entrepreneurial insights have been dissected and demystified, are to develop a structure and strategy to maintain that success.

Part 2: Demystifying Past Success

Once the business starts taking off, the factors that brought success tend to become institutionalized into a rigid strategy and structure. That dampens, not enhances, future growth.

Unleashing Strategy and Structure

Ask family business owners why they have been successful and you will likely hear, "We found just the right strategy at just the right time." When you ask them to describe that strategy, they tend to talk about how they always get in before 7:00 a.m. and work until 10:00 p.m. or about their innovative product line. These may, indeed, be contributing factors to their success, but they are not strategic factors at all.

That doesn't mean such entrepreneurs don't have a strategy. It's just less conscious and less clear in their mind at this phase. By definition, every business has a strategy—whether people know it or not, whether it's good or bad, whether people can explain it or not. The mere existence of the business means there is a strategy. Sometimes the strategy is brilliant. It's something the entrepreneur learned through trial and error and intuitive insight.

But **because entrepreneurs may not be fully aware of their strategies and their important ingredients, they may become confused about their reasons for success.** That's why when someone asks them about their strategy, they talk about their own qualities or philosophies. **The danger of lacking clear understanding of why a business succeeds is that an entrepreneur may cling to every business policy and structure and every personal trait** for fear that changing *any* aspect of how the business is run might destroy success. "If it ain't broke, don't fix it," is the operating philosophy.

Dissecting, demystifying and demythologizing implicit strategies identifies true contributions to success as well as factors that may no longer work (and actually could be dragging the company down) in today's market.

A particular strategy or structure may have been right for the circumstances as the business experienced initial success. Yet as the company enters Phase 2 of the typical family business strategic path and as times change, owners who have not isolated the ingredients of their success tend to institutionalize every minute detail of their behavior and their initial, successful strategy and structure. They further bog down the business in policies and procedures that ensure the company doesn't veer from its original path.

Other inhibitors of change in family firms include:

- Institutionalization of operating details and specific behaviors;
- Deeply entrenched values;
- Long tenures by each generation of leaders;
- Long-term loyalty to managers and advisors;
- Autocratic/paternalistic management style;
- Insulation from changing conditions outside the business; and
- Tendency to be risk- and debt-averse.

These traits have their advantages. But they can also inhibit change. Entrepreneurs often have invested everything in their company. Once success hits, instinct makes owners want to cling to their winning structure and strategy. But what brought a family business its early success may not ensure its future. The family keeps changing. Technology keeps evolving. Markets keep maturing. Competitors keep competing and new competitors enter the fray. If the business doesn't respond and transform, it will lose ground.

Loosening Rigid Strategies

Sometimes the damage is not apparent for years. Market share, return on sales and return on investment are increasing in Phase 2. Things seem great. Nothing seems impossible. Why fiddle with a winning formula?

For one thing, market share will surely top out at some point. Margins will be pressured. Others will find better ways of doing what you do. And then, winning formulas will become losers. Second, while success is mounting, the ingredients to future problems and decline may already be slipping in:

☛ *A homogeneous management team is focused on implementation and keeping up with current growth.* Often a team built to implement one strategy will be unable to embrace, let alone develop or implement, a new strategy. The owner of one company that sells one very successful product through an independent distribution network decided it was time to better utilize that network by acquiring other companies that produce other products for the same market. The sales manager kept saying, "No, we just need to sell more of what we already produce." The financial vice president, who'd been financing growth through cash flow, was adamantly opposed to taking on significant debt that acquisitions would require. Despite its terrific track record to date, the management team clearly is unprepared to adapt to the new vision or move the company in this new strategic direction.

☞ *Fear, intense demands and mistakes make the entrepreneur extremely self-reliant and autocratic.* Such an entrepreneur will seek out and latch on to any source of stability and peace available. This is an understandable reaction to a situation the entrepreneur is less able to control. The natural tendency is to work harder, take more control, retrench and do all the things that are most likely to make the organization unable to make the transition that's required. These inclinations are bound to further undermine creativity and change.

☞ *Loyalty is treasured.* Turnover can be traumatic for entrepreneurs. How dare anyone leave? How dare anyone challenge the strategy? That attitude is counter-productive. It is bound to further alienate and aggravate key employees who may be even more inclined to bail out when the owner stifles their input and authority.

☞ *The entrepreneur invests his or her entire self into the business, often neglecting time with the family.* Tireless commitment demanded by a business' launch and growth becomes a habit that continues even when it becomes less of a necessity. Moreover, entrepreneurs sometimes feel more comfortable at their businesses than they feel with their families. The result can be a weakened foundation of rapport and give-and-take between the entrepreneur and his or her children. When new business strategies are required, entrepreneurs and their successors can be uncomfortable with the necessary negotiations and can find themselves in a frustrating stalemate.

Rather than succumb to these temptations, far-sighted business owners and entrepreneurs stress:

☞ *Organization.* As one company's factories expanded from five to eight, future success grew more dependent on its ability to better organize and coordinate production facilities. In the past, each factory was treated as a separate unit. The second-generation owner is in the process of reorganizing to treat all facilities as a unit, and has created a new position of executive vice president who will report to the CEO and to whom the plant managers will report. The marketing department, which in the past operated on strict production goals, has had the attitude, "If we get enough sales, the rest of the company will take care of getting profits." To gear sales and marketing people toward profitability, the pricing function has been moved from the chief operating officer's office into marketing. New product development is now being integrated into marketing in addition to its historical focus on production.

☞ *Underlying values.* Periods of intense change are good times for owners to consider why growth is so important. They should consider why they are operating the company and whether it is time to sell or whether it's important to keep the business in the family. It's good to take a new look at values and re-articulate them and reassess how the company measures success.

☞ *Openness, reduction of secrecy.* Many owners hold financial information close to the vest. At the family business in the process of reorganizing that we mentioned above, the CEO kept profit figures even from managers of profit centers. Now the family is beginning to meet and share more information — including a conceptual picture of the reorganization. They are learning to share preliminary ideas with key managers, getting input earlier in planning and decision-making processes.

☞ *Competencies, not products.* Once the market for a hot product has been saturated, or tastes or technology change, evaluating what organizational strengths contributed to the companies initial success makes sense. This does not require abandoning the company's traditions. Instead, the company uses its traditional culture to build an appreciation of change and innovation.

Keeping business structure and strategy fluid allows flexibility to respond to new opportunities and react to unexpected threats. Many owners fail to see that their willingness and ability to take a new approach to a commercial or consumer need led to early success more than any particular structure or strategy they built to support that new approach. Future success may well depend on their ability to find yet new and different business ideas, and develop new (and flexible) structures and strategies to support those ideas.

Making Change Part of Tradition

As changing times require new approaches to business, leaders must become champions — not challengers — of change. When a second generation family business found itself becoming bureaucratized, family leaders found a way to move forward by emphasizing a different part of the past they could all rally around. The founder had loved tinkering with machines to find a better way to manufacture products. He was fond of saying, "There's always a better way." His sons and grandchildren used that piece of tradition as a theme for the company's mission and strategy. They demystified the source of the company's success by emphasizing not the founder's genius or particular achievements, but attitudes, values and philosophy.

"As changing times require new approaches to business, leaders must become champions — not challengers — of change."

This illustrates that tradition and change are not mutually exclusive. Here's another example:

Warren Featherbone Co., based in Gainesville, Georgia, has made change an integral part of its tradition. Throughout more than a century of its history, the company has found ways to adapt its products and processes as changing technology rendered its primary products — first "featherbones" (corset stays made of turkey quills), and then plastic baby pants — obsolete. Rather than fighting change, Warren Featherbone went with it. First, competitors introduced plastic corset stiffeners. The company could no longer compete based only on its patented "featherbone" stiffeners. So the company used the new material to develop plastic baby pants in 1938, replacing heavier, hotter rubber pants. Later, disposable diapers cut into that market. The company responded by developing a line of "diaper dress-ups," fancy coverings for the new, popular disposable diapers. After developing a full line of toddler wear, the company became the sixth largest children's apparel maker in the U.S.

The company distilled its family business experience into seven fundamental values: creative thinking; finding a need and filling it; focusing on value for customers; focusing on people at all levels of the process; working hard; maintaining enthusiasm; and maximizing the company's ability to adapt.

The following two exercises should help owners, working with other family business members and shareholders, stretch the boundaries that may limit future success. At the next management or family meeting, owners might consider scheduling time on the agenda to work through these exercises.

EXHIBIT 2 ▪▪▪▪▪▪▪▪▪▪▪▪▪▪▪▪▪▪▪▪▪▪▪▪▪▪▪▪

Exercise A: Reexamining Your Company's History and Lore

- Recall and retell stories about the challenges the business has had to overcome since its inception.

- Instead of emphasizing the founder's or multiple ancestors' genius, strength or other awesome traits, look for instances where the company had to change.

- Describe success as a "group insight" or a "lucky break." The moral should not emphasize the founder's qualities, but the resilience, flexibility and value of change in the business.

- Rephrase any slogans that have been handed down from previous generations, to demonstrate traits such as creativity, energy and flexibility instead of tradition. For instance, instead of the slogan, "A good salesman will deliver it himself," how about "A good salesperson finds solutions to customer's problems." The value of service is preserved, but the updated slogan inspires more creative ways to provide it.

EXHIBIT 3 ▉▉▉▉▉▉▉▉▉▉▉▉▉▉▉▉▉▉▉▉▉▉▉▉▉▉▉▉

Exercise B: Depersonalizing Your Company's Success Factors

Look for ways to stretch past boundaries. Do you make beef jerky or processed food? Are the customers you target hunters and hikers in New England, or potentially outdoors people all over the world? Was past success based on the founder's insistence on "never borrowing a dime," or "frugal cash management" (that might allow the company to assume some debt)?

- What products do you make?

- What product or services could substitute for yours?

- What markets do you serve?

- What are advantages and disadvantages of broadening market definition?

- How do you produce and deliver your goods and services?

- How do competitors produce or deliver differently?

Moving Forward

Holding the company hostage to a rigid structure and strategy, no matter how successfully they worked in the past, is likely to result in a stagnant business with unexciting future prospects. As we will see in the next section, as a company reaches Phase 3, its initial strategy can either limit future growth or unleash a new wave of success. The outcome depends a great deal on how the company defines itself and its strategy.

Part 3: Preventing Past Business Strategy from Limiting Future Success

Paradox: How you define your business and what brought it success determine your ability and freshness to see new ways to do business. A narrow definition of the business and its success factors can lead to paradigm paralysis.

Many family firms are trapped by their past success. Their early strategies are so powerful and so deeply ingrained that change is all but impossible. Moreover, entrepreneurial founders are often highly creative and charismatic, which can easily melt successors' self-confidence to fight for dramatic change.

This section describes ways out of this trap. The first involves looking at the business through a different lens to help redefine the business itself. Second, we offer ways to get over resistance to planning. Next are ways for developing strategic skills. Last comes practical ideas for making change less threatening.

Just What Business Are You In?

In the 1950s, fourth-generation Sam Johnson Jr., became the first new-products director of Racine, Wisconsin-based S.C. Johnson & Co. As he has explained many times, when he developed his first prototype for a new home insect killer, his father scoffed at the idea, commenting, "Don't you know we don't make any product without wax in it?" Sam Jr. offered to put some wax in the formula, but acknowledged that wouldn't improve the product. His father insisted, "What's better about it than the competition's products?" Sam Jr. realized it wasn't, but went back to the drawing board. After further research, he realized existing insecticides were solvent based, which not only smelled horrible, but also killed nearby house plants. He reformulated the product using an effective water-based system that was safe for plants and had a less offensive odor. The result was Raid House and Garden Insecticide, now the world's leading product in its category.

The lessons father and son elicited from the process helped redefine their business. Father realized the company wasn't, in fact, in the wax business; the company's genius was packaging industrial products for consumer markets. The company had a second paradigm shift—from industrial products for consumer markets to consumer products. This enabled Johnson to further expand its product line into outdoor leisure goods, men's grooming aids and women's shaving and skin products. Sam Jr. did so based on the lesson his father brought home: "If you're going to get into a new field, you have to have a better product."

The point: **How one defines what initially brought the company success can limit future success.** Had Sam Sr. insisted that all products contain wax because the company was in that business, it would have remained within that narrow parameter.

Another example is one second-generation manufacturing company that was failing to meet its delivery schedules. The founder took pride in his sales staff, who were so focused on providing excellent customer service that they would make deliveries on their way home if required. That caused the operations people to ignore delivery problems because they saw customer-service as a function of the sales force. It also caused sales people to spend too much time on customer calls, and too little on sales calls. When the founder's son suggested making changes that would solve the problem, his father insisted, "That's not how we do things here." He was clinging to tradition because he believed the sales force's renown customer service was the secret to the company's past success. Had he been able to shift his perspective, to see great customer service as an important success factor, but not necessarily tied to the sales force, he would have been more open to make necessary changes that would solve his delivery problems.

Getting Over Resistance to Planning

Many entrepreneurs hate formal planning. They have built successful businesses without it. They favor action over talking. They live in the present, convinced uncertainty makes it impossible to predict and plan for the future.

But our experience shows that planning is critical for long-term success. For owners who intend to perpetuate their family business, planning is among the most important skills. Specifically, the business' strategic plan and the family's succession plan are essential to ensure future business endurance and health. But planning does not have to be as painful or require as much time or money as many business owners expect. In fact, many business owners misunderstand what planning is.

Many business owners who hate to plan point to reasons that don't hold up under scrutiny. Table 4 shows how owners can reframe their attitudes and assumptions about planning.

TABLE 4 ————————————————————————————————————

REFRAMING ASSUMPTIONS ABOUT PLANNING

PERCEPTION	REALITY
Planning:	**Planning:**
■ limits flexibility	■ expands flexibility
■ is useless with so many uncertainties	■ helps firms anticipate and cope with uncertainty
■ requires owners to share sensitive information	■ empowers organization with more responsibility, commitment and understanding
■ exposes management's mistakes and areas of incompetency	■ allows management to improve skills
■ implies change that can threaten past strategies	■ helps owners and managers base decisions on current and future circumstances, not on past factors that may no longer be relevant

Owners may believe that planning limits flexibility—that they would be held hostage to any five- or even one-year strategic agenda to which they might commit. What if new opportunities or obstacles arise? A plan is just a road map. If a road becomes full of pot holes, travelers can take a detour. If the destination itself burns down, they can turn back or chart a new course. The point is, a plan — even if it is written, signed and circulated — can, and should be re-evaluated as circumstances warrant. In fact, it's important to scrutinize a strategy periodically even if circumstances don't seem to require it. A plan is essential for making the best choices for the future. Without a plan, the business is likely to miss interesting and profitable opportunities and shifts.

Similarly, many owners insist that planning is futile given uncertainty — the likelihood that assumptions and goals are bound to be foiled by the breathless pace of changes in the industry, technology, economy or by family and business circumstances. Yes, uncertainty may cause a plan to become outmoded soon after the ink dries. But the plan itself is not as important as the process of planning. During that process, owners take time to evaluate and analyze their world. Members of the management team learn and think more. Owners who don't plan are less likely to take time to assess the internal and external issues of today. **The process of planning forces owners and managers to keep their fingers on the pulse of their family, business, industry and the world. That's why the presence of uncertainty makes planning more, not less, critical.**

Many entrepreneurs prefer to create ambiguity, thinking that gives them the greatest flexibility. In fact, owners who plan do not sacrifice their prerogative to change their mind or heart; plans enhance that prerogative by helping owners make informed adjustments to their course. Owners also perceive that there is a contradiction between doers and planners. They think doers act and planners ponder. In truth, doing without planning is like leaping without looking.

Other reasons owners resist planning are based on fear — fear of failure, of external accountability or of confronting sensitive family issues. Changes in the family, the industry or the economy that challenge yesterday's strategy, are not a reflection on the owners' competence or people's willingness to respect their position and experience.

The process of planning forces owners and managers to keep their fingers on the pulse of their family, business, industry and the world.

For owners who seriously doubt their families can non-defensively and collectively discuss the business issues, planning can be a truly risky business. However it's all the more important for those families to begin to address those issues. In such cases, start by strengthening the family's ability to communicate and resolve conflict. It may help to refer to previous books in the **Family Business Leadership Series:** *How Families Work Together*; and *Family Meetings: How to Build a Stronger Family and a Stronger Business.*

Developing Strategic Skills

To make strategic change the company's tradition requires leaders to become adept at four strategic skills:

☛ *Perpetual planning.* Every strategy, process, policy, structure and tactic must be put on trial. Leaders must challenge assumptions, test their internal validity, and stretch their boundaries.

One powerful indicator of a business' future health is the number of "strategic experiments" it conducts. "Strategic experiments" are incremental changes such as giving customers more service, exploring new markets or altering how business is done. At any given time, a business usually should have three to six modest initiatives underway based on the company's strategic goals and values.

A commercial printing company with a nice market share in the corporate brochure and marketing material business is stretching its thinking with two experiments: It's using some of its digital reading equipment to create graphic videos. It's also testing a new printing format that simplifies mass mailing for its customers.

☛ *Building an innovative, adaptable organization.* Chances are, the next good strategic idea won't come from today's owner. Even if —in fact, especially if — the owner is the architect of the last brilliant strategic idea, he or she is unlikely to think up the next one. The developers of one idea and strategy tend to become attached to their creations, and have a hard time accepting new ones.

That's just what happened to a successful linen supply firm we know. The CEO broadened the firm from napkins, tablecloths and uniforms for restaurants into laundering uniforms for food processing plants. Dedicated to exploring that idea, she didn't imagine the same opportunity for laundering uniforms for health care clinics. The vice president of production had a neighbor who was the controller of a clinic chain and overheard him complaining about the cost of service. The CEO immediately realized the VP's complaint represented an opportunity to expand into the health care market. She poked fun at herself for not recognizing it before, as her husband is an M.D. in the same clinic!

☞ *Constant reinvestment.* What's the size of the company's strategic investment? Does it have one? Most companies don't or at least don't think they do.

A strategic budget dedicates funds for improving the business' market share, not holding onto current market share; strategic budget expenditures have a pay-off not in the current year, but in future years. Therefore, fixing a leaky roof or replacing a worn-out truck are status-quo investments. But some operating expenses may actually be strategic investments, such as R&D, product development, or investing in a sales person with a two-year pay-off.

Exhibit 4 shows an example of what a strategic budget might look like.

EXHIBIT 4 ▉▉▉▉▉▉▉▉▉▉▉▉▉▉▉▉▉▉▉▉▉▉▉▉

Sample Strategic Budget

New product development	$ 300,000
Expanded plant capacity	$ 1,500,000
New Salespeople	$ 200,000
Training for successor and independent directors and executive management	$ 90,000
Acquisition research and planning	$ 60,000
Board fees	$ 60,000
Shareholder meeting expenses and internships	$ 40,000
Total strategic budget	$ 2,250,000
Net operating profit before depreciation and strategic expenses	$ 6,750,000
Strategic Budget/Funds Available	33%

Non-strategic uses of funds include taxes, dividends, debt repayment, and capital to replace old assets

Reinvesting money in the business to generate future growth is one of three options for directing the cash flow a company generates; the other two choices are to pay out cash flow to owners in the form of dividends or to let it accumulate as retained earnings. The ratio of how much owners invest in strategic initiatives to how much they take out of the business is another powerful indicator of a business' future health. Family stockholders and board members should keep a sharp focus on this.

Exhibit 5 ▮▮▮▮▮▮▮▮▮▮▮▮▮▮▮▮▮▮▮▮▮▮▮▮▮▮▮▮

Strategic Budget Ratio

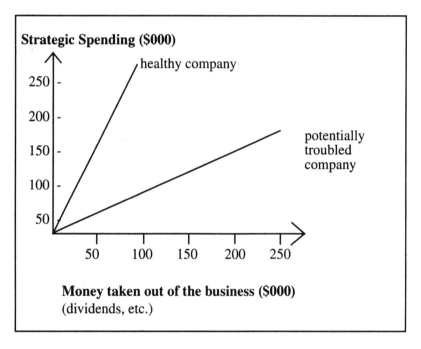

Owners taking out more than they put into strategic investments in a given period is a sign of trouble ahead. Managing the ratio is a very important barometer of a company's future health. The many stories that regularly appear in the business press about a company in bankruptcy often reveal that even as earnings per share were sliding, the company's dividends per share kept rising.

One family business was growing modestly and ran a tight ship, keeping costs down. Its leaders couldn't understand why it was losing market share. The company was devoted to paying shareholders a regular dividend. Over the last five years, that dividend came to 233.8% of its profit. Book value per share, which was $4.55 in 1991, had shrunk to $3.66 by 1996. Because they'd never bothered to do the math, they didn't realize that family members were essentially liquidating the company! Needless to say, the business was ill-prepared to invest in the strategic projects that might generate future cash flow to cover future strategic investments and produce healthy dividends.

☞ *Motivation and commitment.* Aging entrepreneurs have a difficult time sustaining their risk taking. Having achieved much, they may be looking for more personal security and time. But continuous development of the business requires that risk-taking initiatives can't slow down. In fact, in today's world they probably have to increase. **What motivates an already successful entrepreneur to keep wanting to grow, change and devote his hours and passion to the business? We think it's his or her enthusiasm for constant improvement and eagerness to receive constant feedback. The best business owners we know make themselves accountable to demanding external standards and take great personal pride in getting better and better.**

Making Change Less Threatening

Earlier, we recommended that current owners depersonalize the success and vision of the business. Successors need to do the same thing when they are trying to create a culture of strategic change. Instead of submitting new programs as personal ideas, new ideas are more likely to be accepted and effectively implemented if they are seen as collective products to which many have contributed and committed.

No matter how brilliant successors may be, their success will depend on their ability to solicit many ideas from a lot of people. Sharing the spotlight lessens the likelihood

The best business owners we know make themselves accountable to demanding external standards and take great personal pride in getting better and better.

26

that an idea will become charged with other issues, causing the generations to lock horns.

For instance, one successor believes sales force compensation should be switched from commissions to salaries. The current commission-based system was Dad's brain child. Dad founded the business and was its most successful salesman in the early days.

The first step toward change may involve surfacing disturbing data. For instance, sales may be declining and the ratio of new to existing customers has also decreased significantly. Nontheless, inflating product prices and a smaller sales force may still be still leave sales force income about the same.

In step two, the successor could form a task force to look at the information and begin to talk about the need for change. They can be charged with tracking the amount of time salespeople spend with old versus new customers and prospects in each territory or for each product line, to try to uncover any correlation. Successors can have other employees develop reports with data that highlight an issue that needs to be addressed. They may also check with the industry association for any studies on how different compensation structures affect sales.

As the task force starts to suggest ideas, the successor can reinforce members by bringing in an expert to speak to the issue at a meeting attended by the current leader. The expert could be a compensation or industry consultant, a board member or a professional advisor such as a CPA.

TABLE 5

HOW TO DEPERSONALIZE CHANGE

1. Surface disturbing data.
2. Form investigative task force.
3. Seek expert opinion.
4. Share concern with others, like board members, advisors and key executives.
5. Start a small experiment with a different approach.
6. Applaud the company's "tradition of change" exemplified by the founder or predecessor.

Fourth, the successor could bring up the issue at a board meeting — without taking a position. At the meeting, the successor can encourage brainstorming and solicit ideas about ways to motivate salespeople to spend more time with prospects and new customers.

Step five may involve a small experiment with the successor's idea. The successor may suggest salary-based compensation for the two newly hired salespeople and see how it works. Or try it with people in one territory or with one product line.

The hope is that by decreasing the risk and the emotional baggage that comes with successors charging in with new ideas, those ideas will be deemed less threatening. Sprouting from within the organization also serves to rally support from people in other functions and levels.

In this case, another dimension of introducing change in an unthreatening way involves the concept we introduced earlier, making change the tradition of the organization. The successor needs to reframe the founder's contribution to the business from "the person who created a successful commission-based sales force" to "the person who encouraged salesmen to spend more time with customers," which was novel in the industry at the time. **So the focus is on the founder — not as the creator of a specific program or vision, but as an innovator and introducer of something the market had never seen before. That aligns current suggested change with a tradition the previous generation began. In this way, the successor is able to preserve tradition**. But the tradition becomes one of change, rather than one based on a specific task.

Also consider taking advantage of the regenerative power of ideas from the outside world. Successors would be wise to arrange to go places with the older generation owners and leaders, where other people are talking about some of the changes successors would like to implement. This could be a seminar or a visit to another business. The successor of one family retail grocery business wanted to change the format of the stores' eat-in food service section. Father resisted, arguing, "Our food-service is already profitable, so why make changes?" The successor convinced Dad to at least visit other stores that had different kinds of formats, and guess what? The father became excited about many of the new ideas they saw.

Moving Forward

As we will see in the following section, the family business entering Phase 4 confronts competing needs of the incumbent leader, successors and the organization itself. Part 4 explores how current leaders can balance their own needs with the needs of other family business stakeholders and the business.

Part 4: Responding to Family and Business Needs

As the business and the family members mature, their needs, expectations and goals may conflict. The current leader must sort through and address these needs.

If the next generation of family business members comes of age before the owner has successfully navigated the business beyond potential Phase 3 stagnation, the challenges of Phase 4 can be especially stressful. At a time when there are fewer financial and emotional resources to spread around, more family stakeholders show increasing interest in the business and make demands on the business leader. Current owners will more effectively respond to business and family needs if they build strength in five areas:

- family values;
- personal financial security;
- matching family factors with business strategy;
- appreciation of different people's risk tolerance; and
- sense of stewardship.

The Power of Family Values

Integration of family and business needs can create problems. It can also create an uplifting and enriching opportunity to get the family working together by focusing on how the business can reflect and operate on core family and business values. Emphasizing core values tends to help the family rally together.

Many family businesses don't feel bound by a formal approach to strategic planning, which focuses on maximizing shareholder value at an appropriate level of risk. Families tend to use their businesses to pursue a broader range of goals. A deeply shared spirit of entrepreneurship is the basis of some families' business culture and family values. One 68-year-old family business founder decided to give each of his two sons an advance on their $5 million inheritance. He suggested that each find a worthy business to acquire and manage. In this way, the sons could identify growth opportunities, diversify the family's assets, develop as businessmen and maintain the family's entrepreneurial spirit.

Other families use the business to pursue idealistic goals. Since its founding in 1946, the motto of Highlights for Children , Inc. (whose main product is the famous magazine for children) has remained, "Fun with a purpose." That creed has guided three generations of business decisions. No matter how much a new marketing scheme, editorial project or business venture might potentially add to the bottom line, if it doesn't provide children the opportunity for enjoyable learning, it is rejected.

The combination of family and business goals can produce enviable success, particularly when the family is unified around clear values. Shared vision, values and commitments enhance business success. In the book, *Corporate Cultures* (Addison-Wesley, 1982), Terrence E. Deal and Allen A. Kennedy point out, "Companies that do the best over the long haul are those that believe in something." James Collins and Jerry Porras, authors of *Built to Last: Successful Habit of Visionary Companies* (New York: HarperBusiness, 1994) put it another way: "Visionary companies pursue a cluster of objectives, of which making money is only one. . . . They're guided by a core ideology — core values and sense of purpose beyond just making money."

For instance, the fourth generation owners of a scrap yard increasingly see themselves as recyclers who are saving the environment. The founders started out at the turn of the 20th century sorting garbage for valuable parts. During World War I and World War II shortages of metal for war effort, the second generation became recyclers of metals, doing their part to save democracy. By the 1970s, when environmental concern heightened, third and fourth generations continued to do what the companies had done all along, but their kids saw them as heroes who were saving the environment. The conservation ethic existed in scrap dealerships from the beginning, but was called different things at different times and required different approaches.

Each generation approached the family business with new enthusiasm, fueling new energy and insights. These family members were able to draw on their shared values to nurture evolving strategic business advantages.

Reducing Personal Financial and Emotional Insecurity

As important as change is, it can feel, and actually be, risky. In many cases the larger risk comes from avoiding necessary change. **But**

strategic change should be structured to minimize threats to the senior generation's financial and emotional security.

In Phase 1 of the typical family business strategic path (please see Part 1), the startup business sometimes can barely afford to pay the founder a living wage, let alone begin to provide for future retirement needs. During Phase 2, the business owner can afford to draw a good salary, but may not yet be able or inclined to worry about the future. While the company is stuck in Phase 3, retirement may be the last thing on the owner's mind.

However, financial security often becomes especially important during Phase 4, when family and business may compete for limited capital. Just as the business may need to invest in new equipment, technology or people, family shareholders may need cash for college, weddings, or down payments on homes. At the same time, the senior generation's retirement looms nearer. The parents, whose main asset is often the family business, have the most at stake.

The next generation may have gained the experience to assume a greater leadership role and be eager to discuss future succession. Parents who have little, if any, wealth outside the business are likely to feel threatened by the prospect of letting go. They can't afford to. Successors may have lots of energy and ideas for geographic or product expansion. Risky new ventures are the last thing on the incumbent leader's mind. The result is often conflict, which can undermine the family and the business.

Personal financial risk can be reduced if the senior generation builds comfortable "nest eggs" outside the business. Those who have outside financial resources are more likely to take a long-term perspective, not just try to maximize the last five or ten years of their working career. They'll be more comfortable with business risk-taking because their financial future does not depend on the outcome of those risks. Financial independence may also make them willing to allow their children in the business to try new strategies and assume more responsibility and authority.

The senior generation should assess the financial liquidity and cash flow needed to ensure financial security for the business and their future retirement, fund estate taxes, buy out shareholders who want to exit, and fund family life styles and special needs. Some techniques owners can use to become financially independent of the business are explored thoroughly in the **Family Business Leadership Series #7,** *Financing Transitions: Managing Capital and Liquidity in the Family Business.*

33

The easiest way to reduce emotional risk is to introduce change incrementally, step by step. When any employee — family or not, management or staff — comes in with a new idea, the choice need not be all (fund it and gallop off in a new direction) or nothing (reject it out of hand). The organization would be wiser to move slowly in a few new directions, to see which ones work under which circumstances. This is what we call strategic experimentation (please see Part 3). This makes change more palatable both emotionally and financially. It promotes continuous small changes rather than dramatic shifts in direction.

Another strategy for becoming more emotionally tolerant of change is for the parent generation to develop interests in addition to the business, either in the community or the industry. That might include launching a new business, becoming active in social or charitable activities, or leading a trade group initiative. One founder was appointed a regent of his state's university system. Another business leader, Ramon M. Esteves, Jr., chairman of a 150-year-old, seventh-generation family business, wrote a book for his children and grandchildren living in Europe, North America and South America called *Go Into the City: A Grandfather's Letter To His Grandchildren on the Faith of the Catholic Church* (Vantage Press 1994).

Eric Sauder, founder of Sauder Woodworking Co., the nation's ninth largest furniture maker, devoted his energy to the creation of a farm and craft village that would preserve the midwestern heritage he experienced as a child. His son and successor noted, "I think it would have been a big problem for me if Dad did not have that project. Work and church, that's all he did. How in the world was a guy like that who was in perfectly good health going to retire? The only way was if he had something that was really worthwhile and just as exciting as that business."

When the senior generation leaders increase their exposure to the outside world of activities and ideas, they become less emotionally dependent on the business as their main source of identity. Outside exposure broadens their view and enhances tolerance for change.

An often overlooked contributor to emotional discomfort with change is the incumbent leaders' lack of confidence in the leadership skills or experience of the next generation. Successor development, when it is practiced at all in family firms, is usually a conscious process of teaching the business rather than teaching leadership. Authorities on leadership define it as an almost mystical process of melding a mission with people's motivation to achieve that mission.

Encouraging and assisting future leaders to develop these skills will go a long way to helping the owner feel comfortable with incremental strategic change, much of which the younger generation will ultimately have responsibility for implementing.

Incumbent leaders, troubled with their own concerns about identity, usefulness and security are often unable to assess their successors objectively and accurately. Getting outside assistance in evaluating successors' strengths and weaknesses and readiness can also enhance the comfort of departing leaders. These are important functions board members or consultants can provide.

Table 6

INSPIRING AN EFFECTIVE MISSION

The ability to inspire an effective mission and motivation requires several traits and skills:

- The self-confidence to be willing to assert one's personal agenda;

- Honest self-awareness that enables one to feel confident in one's judgments and convictions;

- Sensitivity to others and their responses;

- The ability to integrate individuals' goals and visions into a group mission;

- An understanding of how to overcome resistance to change.

Matching Family Factors with Business Strategy

Family business owners who ignore family considerations — values, as well as composition, structure, style, personality and culture — do so at the peril of the business and the family. Family factors are integral to a family business' strategic direction. Consider an auto parts company that serves a mid-sized Missouri town. The owners are weighing three possible strategic moves:

- **Strategy One:** Add new services and more products at the current location, particularly catering to the light-duty truck and recreational vehicle markets.

- **Strategy Two:** Open two new locations in Nashville, a growing and currently under-served market.

- **Strategy Three:** Buy a small auto parts distribution business that is for sale in Guadalajara, Mexico that sells to much of Central America.

Now consider three families, and write down which strategy you believe would be the best for each family:

- **Family A:** This family, which includes five children, two sons-in-law, seven grandchildren, has had dinner together every Sunday after church since their father miraculously survived an auto accident 13 years ago.

- **Family B:** The owner has a daughter who's been working for Coca-Cola in brand management for five years and is working on her MBA in marketing. Her brother is also finishing his entrepreneurial studies degree at Vanderbilt. The parents, in their 60s, know that they are eager to work together and appreciate each others' talents.

- **Family C:** The parents are eager to retire to a warm climate and have an ambitious son who is equally eager to take the reins of the business. The parents love to travel and speak Spanish.

Table 7

MATCHING FAMILIES TO STRATEGIES

Which Strategy Fits Which Family?

Strategy 1 *Diversify Product/Service Line* Family ____

Strategy 2 *Open New Nashville Facilities* Family ____

Strategy 3 *Buy distributor for Central America* Family ____

When family business seminar attendees play this matchmaking game, the vote is unanimous: Strategy One for Family A; Strategy Two for Family B; and Strategy Three for Family C. Were your matchmaking results the same? But wait. What about each strategy's value? What if they have different expected financial pay-offs — discounted cash flows (DCFs) — the current worth in dollars of an activity's future cash flow after recovering the initial investment? What if Strategy One's financial value is $2,030,000; Strategy Two's comes to $2,430,000; and Strategy Three is expected to produce $1,280,000? Would that change your opinions? Should such personal considerations influence your choice of economic strategy for the future? Most people stand by their initial choice. And in our opinion they're correct!

A family business strategy must fit well with its family structure, values, interests and strengths. Families A and C are unlikely to realize the higher discounted cash flows projected for Strategy Two. They won't have a strong commitment to make it work if it works against the family's situation.

Families must make their mission, values, plans, and individual needs very explicit. Which areas seem to elicit the most similar responses among family business members? Which areas indicate divergence of feelings? Which areas seem consistent with current strategies? Which areas seem to conflict with current strategies?

The best family business strategies are those that pass all the financial analysis tests, but also "fit" the owning family's personality, structure, and values.

For example, had Family A instead chosen Strategy Two based only on its higher projected future cash flow, the requirement for one or more family units to move and travel would likely have felt disruptive to their close-knit family structure. They may never be able to realize that enticing cash flow assumption.

Certainly, a decision must make business sense. For Strategy Two to work for Family B, the children should be competent enough to each run a site, and the market at the proposed new locations should not be saturated. However, if the owners and leaders personally are much more excited by one good strategy than by another, the family will have a better chance at successfully implementing the strategy they're passionate about and that fits their structure.

Assessing Risk Tolerance of Family Members

Equally important are individual family members' risk tolerances. **Even if owners within a generation share a unified vision of strategic goals, divergent risk tolerances may create conflict that sabotages successful implementation.** Significant differences among various family members' attitudes toward risk can also put a damper on succession. A founder who prides himself on having built a successful company without a dime of debt will resist passing the reins to a daughter or son who have borrowed against the full value of their home to invest in a friend's real estate syndicate.

The nature of risk is a strategic factor requiring family focus. Family businesses that have done a good job of developing information and criteria on which and by which strategic plans are made, do a much better job of developing criteria by which acceptable levels of risk can be managed and communicated effectively. One owner told his son who was a manager in the family business, "I can accept a $50,000 mistake. Anything more makes me nervous and would make me concerned about your judgment and ability." This father was setting clear parameters of risk. The son also realized that overstepping those parameters would make the succession process take longer.

It is imperative to create and educate family and nonfamily managers about how the owners define acceptable risk in disciplined financial terms. For instance, the company will only expand when it has no more than a 1:1 debt/equity ratio. One business owner explained that his criteria for buying another business in his field was that it must be able to pay for itself in three years (his CEO son felt that was impossibly conservative). Others will only take on new challenge if return on investment (ROI) is at a certain level (e.g. consistently 25%). **Whether risk is defined as payback periods or levels of debt, the important point is to try to establish, communicate and agree on specific financial criteria that will guide strategic and tactical moves.** Family business members who can do that will have objective criteria on which to base strategic decisions.

Just as in Phase 3, owners in Phase 4 can fight these new demands or use them to create new opportunities.

Developing Stewardship

Many times entrepreneurs set up their relationship with family and employees on blind faith. They can often be heard intoning, "I've never let you down, stick with me. Don't worry, everything's fine." As the owner begins to address the needs of family employees and shareholders in Phase 4, the owner confronts the challenge of shifting his or her paternalistic attitude and approach to one of informing family members and rallying them around exciting opportunities and new directions. **Enabling transition to occur is the essence of stewardship.**

As the next generation's experience and skills develop, business owners can help them by refocusing the spotlight from themselves to the potential successors. For instance, owners can help transfer customer, vendor and community allegiance to successors by increasing their exposure to such outside constituents. This is a very gracious, unselfish and long-term gesture. But make no mistake: stewardship is also a critical element to the future success of the business.

The concept of a steward includes being a custodian, guardian, or keeper of resources for the benefit of future generations and their constituents. That requires passing on responsibilities and letting go of personal control.

Some entrepreneurs may need to shift from the assertion that "This is my business and I will run it the way I want to," to the belief that "I have been fortunate to have the

Enabling transition to occur is the essence of stewardship.

opportunity to lead and grow this organization, which I built not for myself but to pass on to others." Entrepreneurs in the latter category understand their role includes preparing the next generation to perform as well as, if not better than they did. They feel they have been blessed

39

by their opportunity, but it's not theirs to hold forever.

Entrepreneurs who have this attitude and take these actions find that succession runs smoother. They better prepare their organization for the future than those who do not. **Stewardship is a rare trait in entrepreneurs because of the personal sacrifice, herculean efforts and creative energies they have devoted to the business.** Those leaders who are able to adopt and transmit a philosophy of stewardship tremendously empower others in the business and family to pursue not self interest, but what's best for all. That attitude becomes precious in businesses owned by siblings or cousins.

Here's how one 62-year-old, third-generation business owner acted on his deep feeling of stewardship. This owner loved his time at the helm of his family's 75-year-old business and felt a deep sense of pride in the heritage of the business. He had a great deal of appreciation for the good work employees did during his period of leadership. He felt the business was part of the fabric of the community and wanted with all his heart to see it continue to be successful beyond his time. So he championed three efforts to ensure the company would thrive:

- He institutionalized strategic planning in the organization, to have it be a pervasive process and to train members of the organization to be good leaders of the strategic planning process so that the skill would not be dependent on him;

- In anticipation of his retirement at the age of 65, he developed a succession task force of people from the family, the board of directors and the organization to help prepare everyone for a future change in leadership. He wanted his business to see the change in leadership more as an opportunity for renewal than a threat to continuity; and

- Because he had such strong, deep feelings for the quality of employees who had been with the business for an average of 15 years, he wanted to ensure they would not feel wed to past strategies. He therefore asked the board of directors to accept the role of being strategic catalysts, acting as devil's advocates in challenging the company's strategic assumptions.

Stewardship requires leaders to ask themselves how they can best use the resources they possess. They address that question by constantly analyzing available

Stewardship is all about finding ways to break from the past without breaking the past.

opportunities for using those resources. By doing so, they prepare the family and the business to embrace strategic planning and thinking, and to achieve changes necessary to keep the company viable.

Indeed, stewardship is all about finding ways to break from the past without breaking the past.

Moving Forward

Incumbent leaders must negotiate competing needs and desires of family business constituents and the business itself. Successfully doing so will boost the strategic health of the business currently under their care and position the company to reach Phase 5 - Strategic Liberation and Renewal. In the next section successors learn how to enhance their prospects for future succession by focusing less on their own immediate needs and more on a shared strategic vision and goals, on what they can do for the company, and on depersonalizing disagreements with family members.

Part 5: Strategic Liberation and Renewal

Strategic planning is not necessarily a straight-forward, objective process in a family business. Current and future leaders who understand this spare themselves, their managers and their families considerable frustration.

New Models for Strategic Succession

In the traditional model, a great leader passes the torch to a son or daughter and says, "Now you're the great leader." More and more frequently, we see successors who believe that they, along with other relatives, some nonfamily executives and an outside board of directors should jointly carry the torch. Moreover, they use all kinds of data and share it with all kinds of people more openly than the founder. They accept people's ideas in ways the founder might have thought were weak or unnecessary.

As we saw in Part 1 (please see Exhibit 1), the process shifts from the founder defining a focused strategy (Phase 2), that will eventually limit future growth (Phase 3) and conflict with family needs (Phase 4), to successors ensuring that the organization stays fresh strategically with an infusion of new ideas and efforts (Phase 5). At this point the organization often must pry itself from its dependence not only on a single strategy, but also on a single leader's charisma or brilliance.

Indeed, *Built to Last: Successful Habits of Visionary Companies* authors Collins and Porras note: "A charismatic visionary leader is absolutely not required for a visionary company and... can be detrimental to a company's long-term prospects."

It's not that the leader's charisma or brilliance is not valuable. But as the world and organization grow, the company's boundaries must become permeable enough to allow ideas and information to flow in from outside sources. Collins and Porras contend, "Corporations regularly face the dilemma of how to maintain momentum after the departure of highly energetic leaders (often founders)," a phenomenon they call "Post-heroic leader stall." To avoid that, they recommend, "The last thing you should do is to create a cult of personality. Build an organization that fervently preserves its core ideology in specific, concrete ways."

Maintaining strategic vitality requires a company and its leaders

to risk change and embrace future-focused approaches that are likely to invigorate an organization more than stale, immovable strategies. A strategy based on "the way we do things here" is by definition limiting and is not geared to meeting the company's current competitive needs. Nor is it likely to spark motivation and commitment throughout the ranks. Lithonia Lighting, a division of Atlanta-based National Service Industries, started as a maker of residential incandescent lighting fixtures. It later switched to the fluorescent commercial and industrial lighting market as technology and markets evolved, becoming the largest producer of lighting fixtures in North America. During the commercial construction bust of the late 1980s and early 1990s, however, the former family business was flexible enough to reconsider the residential market. Instead of insisting, "we tried that before and it didn't work," the company recognized that the growing presence of home center stores such as Home Depot represented an attractive market that tends to be counter-cyclical to the commercial construction market.

But it's important to distinguish between strategy, which needs constant stoking, and core values, which need to remain stable. *Built to Last* authors Collins and Porras insist that companies must constantly change their strategy in pursuit of the stable values the companies are built around. "The crucial variable," they write, "is not the content of a company's ideology. But how deeply it believes its ideology and how it lives, breathes and expresses it. ... A visionary company almost religiously preserves its core ideology."

TABLE 8

KEYS TO STRATEGIC RENEWAL

What to preserve no matter what	What to modify in response to change
■ Business values and ideology	■ Business strategy
■ Family legacy and commitment	■ Business structure
■ Development of and advancement of employees	■ Infusion of new, outside managers and directors
■ Quality	■ Technology
■ Service	■ Policies and procedures

Many successors who feel ready to take on new challenges struggle with the older generation. Budding leaders are often eager to try out new ideas and assume more responsibility and authority, and receive more recognition. Just as often, regardless of how thoroughly they have evaluated their ideas or how hard they have worked to earn more responsibility, they meet resistance from the older generation. Potential successors may be vulnerable to one of three pitfalls along the path to strategic succession:

- Pushing succession planning before undergoing strategic planning;

- Making a case for succession based on a sense of entitlement instead of vision, skills and experience; or

- Personalizing disagreements over succession or strategy.

Younger generation members who view and develop their skills and experience in relation to how they can serve the company's strategic goals will be more likely to be taken seriously as potential successors than those who argue for advancement based on longevity of employment or membership in the family. Building strategic goals that both generations can agree on is likely to lessen current leaders' resistance to new ideas and delegating authority, and encourage easing on the reins.

Appreciating Inherent Family Business Advantages

Families who view their businesses as transgenerational commitments are less likely than their competitors to focus strategies on short-term, bottom-line performance. That doesn't mean their bottom line will be smaller. In fact, over the long term, such family businesses enjoy many strategic advantages over their competitors:

☛ *Trust and integrity in relationships:* This is especially advantageous when dealing with partnerships, joint ventures and developing long-term business relationships with customers, suppliers and sources of funds. Rapid rates of change and today's intense competitive pressures for speed, efficiency and flexibility are driving all kinds of businesses to a variety of close working relationships that require foundations of trust, reliability and long-term orientations. Because family firms so often foster such values, they are seen as desirable partners in such ventures.

☛ *Longer-term view:* Family businesses tend to resist managing earnings by cutting costs during economic downturns because their longer-term view makes them patient. Such businesses can make decisions that are counter-intuitive to the current fashion, so when certain businesses become unpopular among investors and acquisitors, family businesses with a long-term view may see the possibilities for future growth.

For instance, one family meat-processing company boasts that its nonfamily business competitors worry about showing consistent profits, and pull in their horns when their commodity costs are high. For instance, when highly cyclical pork prices go up, nonfamily-owned competitors raise prices, which results in some lost market share. The family business makes a longer-term decision to keep its products' prices down, increasing market share — even at the expense of current profits. The family firm knows that its commodity costs will someday come back down and profits will rebound. It can afford to be counter-cyclical, investing in plant expansion, holding onto employees and making other moves judged injurious to publicly-traded companies' financial performance.

Huntsman Chemical has grown to more than $4 billion in sales in one generation through its strategy of buying plants and lines of business from public companies. As *Forbes* magazine explains, "A public chemical company may have to apologize to its shareholders for hanging on to an out-of-favor commodity product line. [The Huntsman] family that owns Huntsman does not have any apologies to make and, to judge from its apparent wealth, seems to be getting the better end of these bargains."

A family can spot an opportunity that requires time to ripen and build a strategy, anticipating no return for 10 years. That's why industries or niches that come with long-term or cyclical payoffs tend to be dominated by family businesses. One family business keeps investing in land to grow oak trees that they'll eventually use to produce wine barrels. It takes 30 years—more than a generation—for acorns to grow into mature oaks and pay off. Another example is Esteé Lauder's son, Esteé Lauder Chairman and CEO Leonard, who has been quoted a number of times saying the company can devote itself to long-term product development projects that take years to pay off because they're a family business.

☞ *Ability to make quicker decisions:* A nonfamily business that is small and entrepreneurial can also make quick decisions, but family companies with clear values and strategies of any size enjoy this benefit. Managers in other companies may fear second-guessing owners.

But in such family businesses, managers — who are also owners — don't need permission to make spot decisions.

☞ *Greater loyalty of nonfamily managers and employees*: This is an advantage only to the extent that owners invest in developing and rewarding employees. When customers bring their cars to be serviced, seeing the same service employees gives them security. That will be more likely to happen if owners make an effort to respond to the needs of their employees.

☞ *Higher commitment by owners and managers to the business:* Owner/managers who are highly committed and hands-on better understand risks in the business. They often have an easier time getting permits and community support because others correctly perceive that the owners' commitment reduces risk.

☞ *Lower cost, patient capital:* Family businesses that have a united, committed and experienced ownership team can actually affect their cost of capital. We call this phenomenon the "Family Effect," and it creates a powerful strategic advantage over nonfamily businesses: the potential to create and increase shareholder value at a higher rate.*

Exhibit 6 ▐███

The Family Effect—Family Ownership as a Competitive Advantage

United, Committed Ownership —-> Lower Cost of Capital
—-> Increased Shareholder Value

Here's how it works. The computation is based on three factors: perceived risk of any family business investment; liquidity; and the degree to which family shareholders perceive the value of the family heritage and control (the Family Effect). If shareholders are fighting, all may begin to worry about the future of the business. If family shareholders are not content with management, compensation or dividends they receive, they may insist on high current returns. Shareholders who are

*The mathematical formula for calculating the value of the Family Effect is outlined in *Financing Transitions: Managing Capital and Liquidity in the Family Business,* by François M. de Visscher, Craig E. Aronoff and John L. Ward (No. 7 in our Family Business Leadership Series.)

informed and who feel like they are part of a united team and who have developed broad commitment to an explicit strategic approach are less likely to feel at risk individually and to demand high current returns.

Most public companies have as their goal increased shareholder value. Period. The diversity of public ownership forces public companies to focus on the lowest common denominator that all shareholders can agree on: a higher current return on investment. That's all they may have in common as owners. Family businesses can build a consensus around other values, like creating career paths for qualified family members, earmarking a percent of sales or profit to charitable causes, or even preserving religious values.

A far-sighted member of the fourth generation of one family business developed measures to quantify how well they achieve their values. "In addition to finance, employee development and other [critical strategic measures], we should be identifying and tracking what I'd call 'stewardship' performance values. And they should go at the top," he informed other family business owners. He suggested that stewardship measures be organized around stakeholder groups including shareholders, employees, community and family. Specific measurable variables include employee compensation and benefits relating to industry norms, profit sharing/pension contributions, contributions to church and community, family employment and leadership opportunities, in addition to traditional measures of return on equity, liquidity and dividends. He recommended that all such variables be quantified, tracked and managed, and that strategic decisions be weighed in light of impacts on all these variables. Associates and family member owners consider the work of this company not just remunerative but meaningful.

Whatever goals and values family business leaders emphasize, their success depends on the degree to which they help other family shareholders understand and buy into those ideas. When business owners present strategic plans to family business stakeholders who feel free to question those plans, they have a forum and a process to discuss and debate those plans, which is likely to lead to explicit agreement on the direction of the business. Roy Richards learned this after he and his brother, Jim, took over Carrollton, Georgia-based Southwire Corp. after their father died in 1985. The Richards brothers, the oldest of seven sibling co-owners, built the producer of electrical cable from $550 million in 1985 sales to $1.9 billion in 1996. To maintain good family relations, Richards says, "I think it is very important that the family agree upon their expectations for how the business will perform. Communication in a family business is the only thing to keep a family or a business together. We've had to talk about hard stuff: who's going to be on the board, how much the CEO makes, what his perks are. We listen to criticism and let the family influence the strategic plan." By informing family members about the business and giving them a forum for contributing their perspectives, Richards generates support for the company's direction. This is a powerful cohesive force for the family and the business.

Maximizing the "Family Effect" requires conscious, planned effort as a business passes through each phase of the family business strategic path and each generation of family ownership. It is in the best interest of the business and the family to make this effort. Good family communication, shareholder education, cultivation of shared interests and fostering awareness of shared values go a long way to boosting the "Family Effect."

Maximizing inherent advantages doesn't preclude being open to change. The point is to embrace change — not random, ill-considered new ideas, but those ideas consistent with the special characteristics of being a family-owned business.

Understanding Inherent Family Business Disadvantages

Many owners rely on their built-in family business advantages to sustain them through the ups and downs of economic cycles and their family's constantly evolving needs and demands. However, there's a flip side to combining family goals and dynamics with business goals and dynamics that can create strategic disadvantages. These disadvantages may not be lethal in the company's early go-go days, but may become a liability as the company grows, its market matures and the business environment constantly changes. Some inherent family business disadvantages include:

☛ *Aversion to risk:* This is a function of family businesses tending to use their own money instead of other people's money to fund growth. Leverage is risk from the financial standpoint. Owners who are not changing and not taking risks are unlikely to sustain an exciting growth rate. As a result, the business becomes less attractive to the next generation either as a career opportunity or as an investment.

☛ *Inflexibility:* When so much power rests in one person who is not accountable and when an owner insulates himself or herself from outside advice, the family business can become rigid and averse to change.

☞ *Less global view*: Family businesses tend to feel more passion for and commitment to local markets and opportunities—unless a taste for travel and an international bias happen to be part of the family's unique make-up.

☞ *Lack of fresh insights*: This stems from family businesses' tendency to have no independent directors, limited external experience and few new key managers from outside.

A company may have

Patience can be a terrific advantage, or it can destroy a business that is so patient it fails to respond to opportunities or threats.

developed into a partnership among family members based on the inherent family business advantage of trusting relationships. But changes in the family or the business climate — like a divorce, emergence of overseas competition, or a new crop of grown children in the business — can turn an advantage, such as a longer term view, into a disadvantage, such as inflexibility. The advantage of being able to make quick decisions can deteriorate into a disadvantage of an aversion to risk. Even a family business advantage can be a two-edged sword. **Patience can be a terrific advantage, or it can destroy a business that is so patient it fails to respond to opportunities or threats.** Commitment to a strategy can give a business a tremendous competitive edge, but if commitment leads to inflexibility in the face of economic change, business will suffer.

Turning Disadvantages into Advantages

A family business in Phase 2 that maximizes its strategic advantages has a better shot at navigating its way to later phases. To get there, business leaders must work with family owners to make explicit agreements about how family goals and dynamics fit with business goals and business discipline. Things break down when a highly educated heir assumes family owners are running their business like a public company and other family members expect special access to jobs, perqs and money. To turn disadvantages into advantages, the family must identify its inherent advantages and disadvantages and focus on getting agreement in the family about how to approach the strategic planning process.

Risk and patience are good examples. At a board meeting, one family member got into a discussion with independent directors about what rate of return the family expected the business to provide. The third-generation family contracting company has been in business for more than 70 years, but its owners never asked themselves that question. Its strategy had been simply to eke by until the next opportunity came along to do a big job and earn a big profit. The family business focused on providing jobs that furnished a decent living for the six family members, keeping employment relatively stable and maintaining quality. Outside directors insisted that was not good enough. They saw the family substituting the interaction of family values and dynamics for market discipline. The family argued that their patience allowed them to still be in business while many competitors had gone bankrupt. The board members pointed out that patience also made them accept a lower rate of return. They calculated that the business' return on investment over 10 years averaged 3% a year; over the same period, investing in bonds would have yielded a 7% annual return, and stocks would have returned 14% annually. Board members explained that the family should expect the return on an illiquid asset such as a family business, which is subject to greater risk, to be closer to 15-18%. The family haggled back and forth, and ultimately agreed to target a minimum 12% annual return. Once they reached this consensus, they were able to discuss how to manage their businesses to reach that level.

What Have You Done for The Family Business Lately?

Consider the different approaches taken by two contenders for the presidency of a janitorial products distributor. Scott, head of purchasing and personnel, was getting impatient with his progress on the ladder. He submitted his resume to his 70-year-old uncle, the CEO and owner. Scott pointed out that he has worked hard for the company for 16 years and should therefore be promoted to a newly created position of assistant to the president. His uncle acknowledged that he works hard and has done a good job, and asked Scott, "What is your vision for the company and why are you the one who should execute plans to get the company where it should be?" Scott got defensive, deflected the first question and answered the second question, "I've earned this promotion. This company should give it to me."

This is not the worst response a potential successor can make — the worst response would be, "I'm a family member, I deserve the job." But his brother, Barry, CFO, had a better approach. Although he has worked at the family business a few years less than Scott, Barry also has a terrific resume highlighting some large projects and people he has managed, and the profits and savings he has produced. He has been more preoccupied with the future of the company than his own future. When his uncle asked about his vision for the future of the company, he answered, "I haven't figured that out yet, but I'm working on increasingly important assignments that will help define the future of the company." Barry is willing to let others judge whether he has the profile that fits the needs of the company. While Scott frets over what the family business can do for him, Barry ponders what he can do for the family business. Guess which brother their uncle designated his successor?

Depersonalizing Disagreements About Succession or Strategy

Arguments about the business between members of different generations are often steeped in deeply personal issues. For instance, one successor takes afternoons off to pick up his daughter at school. The current owner may argue, "You're taking advantage of your position by taking off so many afternoons every week." In reality, the situation may (consciously or unconsciously) dredge up personal feelings such as "You're not as committed to the business as I am," or "Spending so much time with your children makes me feel guilty about not having taken more time helping bring you up." These are arguments no one can truly win. By stripping away the personal layers of a disagreement and focusing on the future, not the past, family members can begin to rally around common goals they can work on together.

Alison, 35, seems to have it all: the title of CEO and a controlling share of stock in the plumbing distribution company her father, now 72, founded in 1954. She also has a problem with her father, a traditional entrepreneur who is still chairman and who relishes his role and his power. One cultural trait the company has retained from her father's tenure is that employees make no independent decisions—they go to the boss and ask. While Alison is on the road about 60 percent of the time, she's not available to encourage employee initiative. Her father, Morty, quite eagerly steps in to make decisions—such as the purchase of expensive new equipment or real estate—effectively, if unconsciously, sabotaging Alison's objective.

Their increased fighting eventually motivated them to hire a consultant skilled in intervention and mediation. The consultant helped them identify strategic goals they agree on, but never realized they shared. For instance, they both believed it was time to hire a team of experienced managers with expertise in marketing, finance and operations. But they were busy fighting over turf (this business is or was mine, and you should do what I want you to do) instead of discussing the company's needs and committing to working together to achieve shared goals. As they continue to articulate and agree upon future strategy, the father-daughter conflicts diminish.

Table 9 _____

ASK NOT WHAT THE COMPANY CAN DO FOR YOU, BUT WHAT YOU CAN DO FOR THE COMPANY

What the Business Can Do For You	What You Can Do for the Business
■ Give me employment.	■ Educate yourself and give yourself experiences that promote the skills and insights that will contribute to and advance the business.
■ Give me money.	■ Control your lifestyle so that your demands on the business will not sap the financial resources it needs to grow.
■ Give me recognition.	■ Foster credibility and support for the business among all family members, and share recognition.
■ Give me power to do what I want to do.	■ View the business as a mechanism through which I can understand the needs and desires of the marketplace and the family, to achieve goals that satisfy all.
■ Give me security.	■ Encourage the business to challenge the status quo for the long-term security of all.

Getting Input from the Outside

Family businesses that reach Phase 5 tend to have one critical resource that those who bog down in Phase 3 or 4 lack: input from the outside. This can be in the form of a board of directors or a management team stacked with people whose expertise, temperament and style are different than those of the owner. Owners should solicit and consider input from outside directors and advisors, inside managers, peers from business networking organizations such as Young Presidents Organization (YPO), The Executive Committee (TEC) or The Alternative Board (TAB), for example. Those who do will likely have an easier time understanding and managing the five phases of the family business strategic path.

Here's how a few business owners solicited input from outsiders with expertise in areas where the companies lack experience:

- One manufacturer chose independent directors known for their skill in strategic planning, and learned how to use economic value-added (EVA) as a way of evaluating existing businesses and potential new businesses. This helped him begin the process of divesting underperforming assets and acquiring potentially lucrative new businesses.

- A real estate company that was struggling with how to define risk used a consultant and his outside CPA with experience in evaluating risk objectively.

- Two new executive hires helped one distribution company's management team understand and better anticipate changes in the industry, allowing the business to move ahead of the change curve rather than consistently playing catch-up. This company also tapped an outside director with experience in creating strategic alliances in the distribution chain. He helped identify greater efficiencies in the distribution channel to be shared with suppliers and customers.

- One newly appointed third-generation leader was eager to apply the latest information and communications technology to his chemical manufacturing company's production and warehousing. He asked his peers in his local YPO chapter for ideas and names of reputable vendors. They offered plenty of suggestions, and also warned him to avoid mistakes they had made — especially the common mistake of applying technology to existing inefficient systems. The advice led him to redesign those systems first, which resulted in substantial productivity gains and savings.

With outsiders challenging current strategic assumptions, strategic issues can be kept on the front burner. **In Phase 5, companies must always pay attention to strategy.** Input and insight from fresh faces reinforces strategic thinking and ultimately makes it part of the culture.

TABLE 10

QUESTIONS TO HELP OWNERS MOVE THROUGH THEIR FAMILY BUSINESS STRATEGIC PATH

Phase	Independent Director	Inside Observer (e.g., spouse)	Own Critic	Advisor/ Consultant
1 Launch	What business are you in?	Are you giving me personal feedback on how I can grow?	Am I proud of how I'm supporting and treating the people who work for me?	Are customers reordering?
2 Demysti-fication	Why are customers buying from us?	Are we attracting new, very talented people?	Am I finding time to expand my professional education?	Who are the most profitable customers?
3 Plateau	How are we investing in new ideas?	Do I feel I'm growing professionally?	Is business fun? Am I spending time in the market, with customers?	Who are the sources of new ideas?
4 Integration	What are the business and personal visions of family successors?	Does the organization respect the successors?	Are family successors eagerly seeking my opinions?	How often does the CEO say "no" to successors' ideas?
5 Liberation	What special competencies are we developing?	What's our mission?	How am I adding value?	How well are we perform-ing on key benchmarks?

55

Moving Forward

Successors who know what to preserve and what to adapt, who can depersonalize disagreements, who can focus on improving the prospects for the business instead of their careers and on developing their own strategic skills and experience, will have an easier time creating credibility and gaining the respect of current owners and management. And that should, in turn, have a positive impact on successors' careers and on the strategic culture of the business itself. These are essential ingredients that will enable family businesses to renew their strategic vitality as they enter Phase 5.

Conclusions
Getting from Here to There

To navigate your way to where you want to go, you need to know where you are now.

Each phase of the family business strategic path brings new benefits and a new crop of headaches. There's little as exciting as the startup phase of a new business, when success is limited only by the vision and energy of the founder. The downside is the struggle to raise capital, to turn a profit and the need to work long hours. The allure of Phase 2 is that the business has caught on and is growing rapidly. But that growth requires more resources, time, structure and people. The same is true throughout the company's development: getting to each new phase represents exhilarating achievement, yet poses new and exasperating problems.

Despite the frustrations, the challenges business leaders face in each phase are normal. Understanding these developmental phases not only helps owners identify the stage their business is in, it also helps them accept that many typical and even predictable pitfalls don't necessarily reflect the founder's abilities. Once owners can depersonalize and predict challenges that lie ahead, they can develop strategies for damage control and for future growth. Owners may not be able to avoid all the problems of each business phase any more than people can avoid life's normal frustrations. However, we hope this book can help family business leaders work through each phase more quickly and avoid reverting to earlier stages.

After all, family business strategic development is rarely a purely linear process. Many family businesses move ahead in fits and starts, then stall due to a business, industry or family snag that causes the business to regress. But by addressing current and future issues before entering the next phase, it is possible to smooth out the process and react with greater insight and speed.

Not all businesses reach Phase 5. Some sell out during the height of Phase 2, before the frustrations of that phase take hold. Some never seem able to develop past Phase 3's rigid structure and strategy, or fail to learn how to resolve the conflicting family and business needs of Phase 4. But long-lasting, very successful companies must go through all the phases.

In Part 1 we introduced Jim and his family, whose computer store chain was stuck in Phase 3, as sales flattened and margins eroded. One of his daughters, who was involved in many volunteer parent-teacher projects at the elementary school her children attended, saw how the school was struggling to best utilize technology. She suggested that the company target schools as a new market. She was excited about the possibility of adopting her children's school and donating equipment to it, thereby creating a testimonial that would spark word-of-mouth.

Her father initially dismissed the idea, based on his vision of the business as a retail chain. The daughter insisted that what made the business successful in the past was not solely the long hours or store locations, but the tremendous service he had always provided customers when they had questions. The board of directors liked the idea of diversifying into new types of markets within its geographical web. That sparked the idea of targeting small businesses as well. The fresh outlook of one of his daughters and the persistence of his board of directors convinced Jim to try out the idea with a few small-scale experiments, which showed exciting potential.

Before rolling out the new strategy, though, Jim, 58, realized he needed to focus on his own personal financial security. He decided to sell a partnership interest in some of his store locations to free up funds for himself and his wife's future retirement as well as for the new business ventures. That helped Jim sail through some of Phase 4's challenges before they developed into severe problems. The daughter's insight made Jim realize she was a viable candidate for future successor. This inspired him to begin investing more time and energy in further developing the leadership skills of his three children in the business and to begin exploring future succession plans.

Like Jim, many family business leaders feel frustrated when they get stuck. Many leaders feel this is a personal reflection on their abilities. The may respond by resisting new ideas and strategies. We hope that this book has convincingly demonstrated that no leader, no matter how brilliant or experienced, can steer a business clear of every developmental pitfall or pothole. By studying our road map of typical challenges and problems that businesses tend to confront at each development stage, leaders can become better prepared to address them, liberate themselves and their business from those challenges and strategically renew their organization.

Appendix: Financial Performance Over The Family Business Strategic Path

EXHIBIT 7

Liquidity

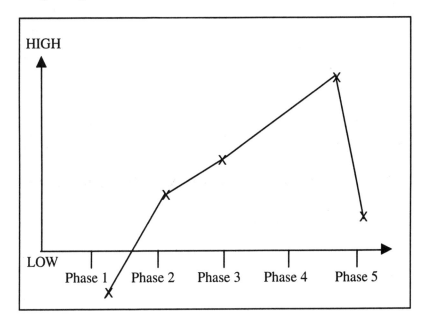

EXHIBIT 8 ■■■■■■■■■■■■■■■■■■■■■■■■

Return on Investment

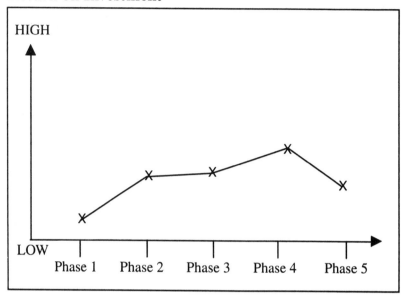

EXHIBIT 9 ■■■■■■■■■■■■■■■■■■■■■■■■

Sales Growth

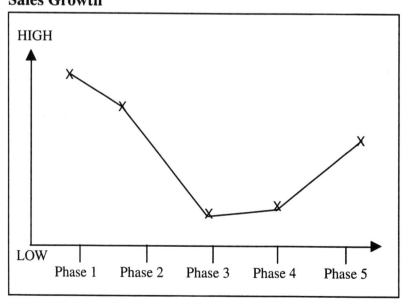

EXHIBIT 10 ▐▬▬▬▬▬▬▬▬▬▬▬▬▬▬▬▬▬▬▬▬

Strategic Budget

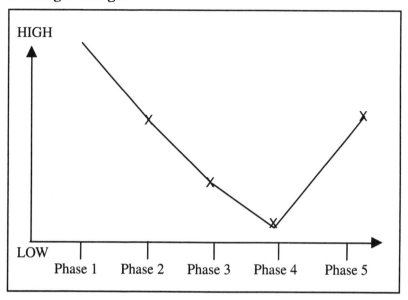

EXHIBIT 11 ▐▬▬▬▬▬▬▬▬▬▬▬▬▬▬▬▬▬▬▬▬

Strategic Experiments

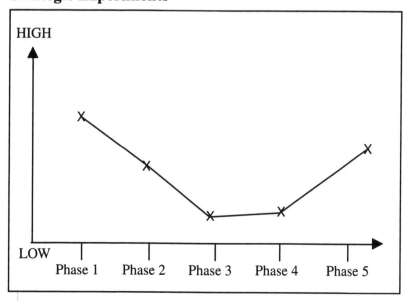

Index

67

The Authors

Craig E. Aronoff, Ph.D.

Co-founder and principal of The Family Business Consulting Group, Inc., Craig Aronoff is a leading consultant, speaker, writer, and educator in the family business field.

As the founder of the Cox Family Enterprise Center at Kennesaw State University in Marietta, GA, Aronoff invented and implemented the membership-based, professional-service-provider sponsored Family Business Forum, which has served as a model of family business education for some 150 universities world-wide. He holds the Dinos Eminent Scholar Distinguished Chair of Private Enterprise and is a professor of management in Kennesaw State's Coles College of Business.

As a consultant, Aronoff has worked with hundreds of family companies in the U.S. and abroad on issues including generational transitions; developing business and family governance processes and structures; finding and articulating family missions and values; facilitating decision making and conflict resolution; managerial development; family compensation and dividend policies; family meetings; and more. As an inspiring, informative and entertaining speaker on a variety of family business topics, he speaks regularly to trade and professional groups and has lectured at over 80 universities.

With co-author John L. Ward, Aronoff is perhaps the most prolific writer in the family business field. He has authored, co-authored or been editor of more than two dozen books, including the 15-volume *Family Business Leadership Series* and is executive editor of *The Family Business Advisor*.

Listed in *Who's Who* and widely acknowledged for his work in the area of family business, Aronoff has received, among other honors: the Family Firm Institute's Beckhard Award for Outstanding Contributions to Family Business Practice; The Freedom Foundation's Leavey Award for Excellence in Private Enterprise Education; and the National Federation of Independent Business Foundation's Outstanding Educator Award.

Aronoff grew up in a family business. He received his bachelor's degree from Northwestern University, his Masters from the University of Pennsylvania, and his Doctorate from the University of Texas at Austin.

John L. Ward, Ph.D.

A co-founder of The Family Business Consulting Group, Inc., clinical professor at Kellogg School of Management and Wild Group Professor of Family Business at IMD, Ward teaches strategic management, business leadership and family enterprise continuity. He is an active researcher, speaker and consultant on family succession, ownership, governance and philanthropy.

He is the author of three leading texts on family business, *Keeping the Family Business Healthy, Creating Effective Boards for Private Enterprises,* and, *Strategic Planning for the Family Business.* He is also co-author of a collection of booklets, *The Family Business Leadership Series,* each focusing on specific issues family businesses face.

Ward graduated from Northwestern University (B.A.) and Stanford Graduate School of Business (M.B.A. and Ph.D.). He is the co-director of The Center for Family Enterprises at Kellogg and currently serves on the boards of several companies in the U.S. and Europe. He conducts regular seminars in Spain, Italy, India, Hong Kong, Sweden, and Switzerland.

John and his wife, Gail, a Chicago high school principal, live in Evanston, Illinois. They have two adult children. They are active in community and educational activities and enjoy family travel and sports.